TWELVE SECRET VOICES
A True World War One Mystery

By
Anne and Damian Ward

Photography by
Rebecca Smith

GSP

Contents

Twelve Secret Voices
Anne and Damian Ward

Published by Greyhound Self-Publishing 2021
Malvern, Worcestershire, United Kingdom.

Printed and bound by Aspect Design
89 Newtown Road, Malvern, Worcs. WR14 1PD
United Kingdom
Tel: 01684 561567
E-mail: allan@aspect-design.net
Website: www.aspect-design.net

All Rights Reserved.

Photography © 2021 Rebecca Smith
Cover Design Copyright © 2021 Aspect Design
Cover photograph © 2021

ISBN 978-1-909219-80-9

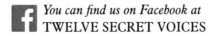

You can find us on Facebook at
TWELVE SECRET VOICES

PREFACE

We are going to tell you about a mystery from the First World War. It is not about a locked box, sealed documents or a handmade trench artefact. For a refreshing change it is a mystery about a.......bedspread.

On 12 November, 2018 we were privileged to find it in a charity shop and during these uncertain times of Covid-19, it has given us a wonderful distraction and an opportunity to talk about something positive while we explored its story and wrote this book.

We hope our story entertains you as much as it has entertained and educated us.

We would like to thank all who patiently answered our questions, gave advice and criticism and contributed in any way to our mystery.

Chapter One

A mystery unfolds

I (Anne) am a hoarder!

I am not ashamed to admit it. I hoard information. I'm very curious about a lot of things. If a subject gets my interest, I love finding out as much as I can about it. And I like to get the right facts. If I see a docu drama or factual history movie, I will look up its subject matter to get more facts and details. My husband Damian is very tolerant of this hoarding of mine. He himself is a great steam railway enthusiast and enjoys researching that. Often if he sees them on television or in print, he will be able to relate a wealth of information. So when I came across this unusual, unnamed, bedspread, it was an incredible 'gift' for someone like me.

I found it on Monday, 12 November, 2018, whilst scouring charity shops for a tablecloth (or large sheet) for a Christmas party. This was to be a very special party as my sisters and their families were coming to our home in Wales from Australia and South Africa. On hearing my query, the British Red Cross shop manageress produced from their back room a large storage bag brimming with white goods. "I'm not quite sure what is in here, but have a look" she said before turning to another customer.

I happily rummaged in the bag of tablecloths and bed sheets. And then I saw something trimmed with lace. Thinking that that would look very smart, I eased it out and unfolded it.

Unfurling before me was and arrangement of white square panels, three across and four down. Each panel was embroidered in its centre with white thread and they in turn were conjoined together with a wide strip of lace. The same lace ran along the outside. "So this is a whitework bedspread", I realized. "How very elegant!" Because it was all in white I had to lift it closer to see exactly what the embroidery was. I was expecting the usual flowers, baskets of fruit or bonneted figures. I was disappointed on that score as none of these were there. So why was I standing there stunned and surprised?

I was looking at a South African springbok that was exquisitly hand embroidered in a regimental badge! And I knew that because I was raised in South Africa and recognised it right away. It was the South African Overseas Expeditionary Force badge. I looked at another panel – that had a Canadian regimental badge embroidered on it and another panel had a New Zealand regimental badge!

It was a bedspread; hand embroidered with twelve different regimental badges from seven different countries – England, Wales, Canada, Australia, South Africa, Ireland and New Zealand! This I knew was very unusal so..........

I walked out the shop with two linen tablecloths and a bedspread!

Chapter Two

So what have we got?

As I had already mentioned, I knew this was Whitework. This is any style of embroidery but done with white thread on a white background. The intended picture is lightly drawn onto the cloth with a pencil and then the needle worker 'filled it in' like you would a picture with pencil strokes. The craftmanship on our bedspread was of very high quality and it must all have taken a very long time to make. Some of the badges are incredibly intricate.

Let us now tell you about the regiments themselves.

Starting from the top left, the twelve regiments and corps depicted on the bedspread are:

1) ROYAL FLYING CORPS

2) ROYAL ARMY MEDICAL CORPS

3) CORPS OF ROYAL ENGINEERS

4) HIS MAJESTYS LAND SHIPS (TANKS)

5) THE WELSH REGIMENT

6) THE ESSEX REGIMENT

7) SEAFORTH HIGHLANDERS OF CANADA

8) AUSTRALIAN ARMY

9) SOUTH AFRICA OVERSEAS EXPEDITIONARY FORCE (1st)

10) ROYAL MUNSTER FUSILIERS

11) KINGS COLONIALS NEW ZEALAND

12) CANADIAN EXPEDITIONARY FORCE

Here Damian picks up the baton:

In the British and Commonwealth army there is an order of precedence, or seniority, of every unit, and every single unit knows its place in the order. The order is based on the notion that the senior part of the army is the cavalry, and then come the artillery, followed by the engineers, then infantry and then the supporting corps. This is the basic structure of the historical order in which the regiments were formed. BUT there are quirks that can complicate things, such as that The Royal Horse Artillery is the senior regiment, but only when on parade with their guns. The Household Cavalry, Cavalry Regiments and Royal Tank Regiment are next and together these form the Royal Armoured Corps. The Royal Regiment of Artillery is next followed by Royal Engineers and then Royal Corps of Signals, The Foot

Guards, Line Infantry, and The Rifles, which all make up the infantry. The next regiment is the Special Air Service and Army Air Corps followed by their support corps.

Now, seniority does not come from when the current regiment or corps was created, but it goes back to the earliest recognised time of formation of that regiment or corps within the Royal Army in England. How does this work? Well – if you look at the Foot Guards, the oldest regiments are in fact the Scots Guards and the Coldstream Guards and you would think that they would rank as one and two in front of the Grenadiers. However, the Coldstream Guards were part of the parliamentary army and the Grenadier Guards were part of the Royalist army, and the regiment that became the Scots Guards (no you can look it up!) were part of the Scottish army, so the Grenadiers are the senior Guards regiment, the Coldstream second and the Scots third.

The order on the bedspread does not follow this, and we have no idea why the badges are arranged as they are so we will give a potted history of each in the order of army hierarchy precedence (well – more or less) as this will make it seem clearer.

His Majesty's Land Ships (Tanks)

So we will start with the Tank badge, even though they were the last force to enter the war.

The tanks main purpose was to break through enemy trenches, destroy barbed wire and barricades and other strongholds. They also transported supplies and troops.

In 1911 an outline design for a tracked and armoured vehicle with artillery was submitted to the British War Office by an Australian civil engineer called Lancelot de Mole. The idea, however, was not new. There is the famous sketch of Leonardo da Vinci's fighting vehicle (circa 1487) and the Russians, French and Austrian War ministries were also looking at designs at the beginning of the 20th century. The tanks potential was put to the British War Office by British Army officers in late 1914 but was not taken further by the BWO as they already had a system with horses and trains of transporting their artillery. The plans were taken over by the Royal Navy as the First Lord of the Admiralty had seen scaled down prototypes being tested and he saw their potential. He, that is Winston Churchill (yes, HIM) set up the Landship Committee in February, 1915.

Little Willie, as the Mark 1 was code named, first saw action on the battlefield in September 1916 at the Battle of Flers-Courcelette. In the press the fleet were heralded as a great success and an asset to the war effort. It also was the great counter attack to the German machine gun. But on the battlefield, they were anything but. Their development had been rushed so as to get them to the front line and have the element of surprise. They were not fully tried and tested and some crew members never actually got to go in one until the day of the battle. It took another year to improve its tactics, fixed reliability issues, handling and operation. And then sufficient numbers had to be built and men trained.

They were maned by a crew of eight – a commander who was also the brakesman, one driver, two gearsman and four gunners. The noise inside was unimaginable and the crews often passed out due to the carbon-monoxide fumes that built up in this enclosed space.

In our research we found two official WW1 tank corps badges but mysteriously neither looked like ours. Even the title HMLS TANK did not seem to exist. This was a strange start!

Today it is the Royal Tank Regiment.

Royal Corps of Engineers

Engineers have been a part of armies since there were such things as armies and defensive fortifications. If you are going to build or attack an enemies defences it's a highly advised to have good builders who have specialist skills. Although the Royal Engineers claim a link back to William I, in fact they can be traced back to the Board of Ordinance in the 15th Century (along with the Royal Artillery). In 1716 the Corps of Engineers was formed but with Commissioned Officers only, with Artificer Companies made up of local labourers and civilian artisans doing the actual work. This situation was not very good as there was no 'uniform' to the items being built, each labour force doing it their way, and in 1772 the first Soldier Artificer Company was formed. 1787 saw them become Royal Engineers and at the same time the Corps of Royal Military Artificers made up of *all ranks* was formed. Its name was changed in 1812 and finally the two were merged in 1855 as the Corps of Royal Engineers. Phew we got there!

World War I saw a massive increase in the range and scope of their work with combat mining and tunnel construction and, depending on the circumstances, constructing the barbed wire defences. Behind the front lines they were responsible for building the support structures, including light railway lines, repairing roads, upgrading bridges, mending tracks, and even being responsible for some of the early gas attacks.

From the start of the 20th century there had been the realisation that aerial reconnaissance would be vital so the Royal Engineers formed balloon squadrons. And these became our next badge.

Royal Flying Corps

They became a separate corps on 13 April, 1912, and had four squadrons.

Squadron one flew hot air balloons.

The other three squadrons had aircraft from the start.

Squadron two became a training unit only, with three and four forming the first reconnaissance squadrons.

There were no specialist fighter or bomber aircraft at the start of WWI. They all were used for aerial observation and the pilots were not equipped with parachutes, but they carried revolvers, rifles and took pot shots at enemy aircraft.

The first fighter aircraft came into service in 1915 – the Bristol Scout – which was fitted with the Lewis Machine Gun.

On April 1, 1918, they were merged with the Royal Naval Air Service and became the Royal Air Force.

As an aside One Squadron RFC became One (fighter) Squadron RAF and my (Damian's) Great Uncle would later serve with them in WW2. A final side-line is that they also flew Harrier Jump Jets and so they took off vertically twice in their history.

These are line regiments, so called because they fought in the line of infantry, and each regiment has a name and number/s. Here is some background to give an idea of their operating system: from the formation of the permanent or standing army each battalion was just given a number, 1st of Foot, 2nd of Foot and so on, and these were formed or raised as wars and crisis needed more soldiers, and then some would disbanded at the end of that war or crisis. The officer would buy their commissions up to the rank of Colonel. This meant that if you were rich and spent enough money you could rise very fast. Not so for the ranks. They had to prove themselves and work their way up.

This system of being able to buy a commanding rank meant that often young, and worse – OLD – unfit and totally unsuitable men ended up in command. This system was kept going until the Crimean War (1853 to1856). It was then finally realised to be 'unfit for service' and 'decommissioned'.

Shortly after this The Indian Rebellion (or mutiny) or the 1st Indian War of Independence of 1857 brought home the fact that India was controlled by the *private army* of the East India Company.

The need for reform was clear but it was only in 1881 that the reforms really started. The line regiments were now given County or a regional identity and each regiment had a name and the numbers from the earlier system.

The next three regiments were all formed in 1881 as a result of these reforms but have had different paths since. So, looking at the bedspread –

Welsh Regiment 41st and 69th Foot

Our first regiment and not entirely Welsh!

Well, the 41st were, but the 69th were South Lincolnshire. (I have no idea who brought them together). The pre-war regiment had two regular full time battalions, a reserve and four part time (Territorial) battalions.

During the First World War the regiment expanded to 23 battalions and saw action across all areas except the African campaigns around what is now Tanzania.

In 1969 the Welch Regiment and the South Wales Boarders were amalgamated to form the Royal Regiment of Wales (29th and 41st Foot)

Today they are the Royal Welch formed in 2006 when they amalgamated with the Royal Welch Fusiliers.

And no, we have not made typing errors with our C's and S's in Welch!

The Essex Regiment 44th and 56th Foot

Now this Essex the 44th was an amalgamation of the East Essex and 56th West Essex.

Like the Welch Regiment they started with 2 regular and 4 territorial battalions and a reserve battalion.

The Essex would expand to 30 battalions for World War One and like the Welch these served across the Western front as well as Gallipoli, Egypt and the desert campaigns.

In 1958 as a single battalion regiment they merged with the Bedfordshire and Hertfordshire Regiment to form the 3rd East Anglian Regiment (16th and 44th Foot) and in 1964 they became part of the new Royal Anglian Regiment.

Royal Munster Fusiliers 101ˢᵗ and 104ᵗʰ Foot

Remember we mentioned the East India Company had their own army? Well, the Royal Munster Fusiliers started out as part of the East India Company as the Bengal European Regiment. They then became 101ˢᵗ (Royal Bengal Fusiliers) foot, or the 1ˢᵗ Bengal European Fusiliers. The other regular regiment was also part of the East India Company as the 104ᵗʰ Foot (4ᵗʰ Bengal European Fusiliers). Both these regiments were composed of white European soldiers and not locally raised Indian Sepoys. These regiments became part of the British army in 1861 when the East India Company's private army was taken over and absorbed into the rest of the British Army.

So where is the Irish connection we hear you ask? Well, that is from Munster Militia regiments that were used to form the regiment in 1881 and these were from Irelands South Cork Light Infantry Militia, the Kerry Militia and the Royal Limerick County Militia.

The 2ⁿᵈ battalion was all but wiped out as part of the rear-guard following the battle of Mons. They were quickly withdrawn, reformed, and appear later in our story.

At the end of the war and following the Irish War of Independence the regiment was disbanded in 1922 along with most of the other British Army regiments (but not the Irish Guards) that had been raised in Eire (Irish Free State).

Royal Army Medical Corps

The medical corps can trace its history back to the start of the standing army when Charles II was restored to the throne. The organisation was really that a regular doctor was assigned to a battle or crisis and given the title of Medical Officer. The first change was in 1793 at the Napoleonic Wars, when the Army Medical Board was created and new purpose built General Military Hospitals were established. The Army Medical Board could not cope with all the sick and wounded and it is worth remembering that far more men died of illness than in battle. At the end of the Napoleonic War in 1815 the board was disbanded and the Office of Director-General was established, headed by James McGigor, and the organisation of medical services for fighting forces was improved and regularised. There remained the problem that the doctors were still not army officers and as time went on recruitment was a major problem. (Aside from the most famous fictional army doctor! Well, that's elementary!)

In 1898 the Royal Army Medical Corps was finally created bringing the provision of organised medical services fully into the army. Now there was a clear system of qualified doctors as commissioned officers and other ranks as medical orderlies.

The Boer War in South Africa greatly highlighted the need for better surgical training and further reforms were put in place just in time for the outbreak of World War One. The corps ran a system of 1st aid posts, casualty clearing stations, field hospitals, hospital trains, base hospitals, and then hospitals back in Britain to cope with the vast numbers of wounded men from the Western Front and all other campaigns. It is worth mentioning the wounded included prisoners of war.

Today the RAMC continues to provide medical care to the British Army.

We have now covered all the BRITISH ARMY badges of the UK and Ireland on our bedspread. Now we go to the international ones!

Seaforth Highlanders of Canada (72nd Battalion)

This is an infantry regiment.

What – back to an infantry regiment! We had said we were now doing line regiments. What's going on?

This Canadian Highlanders battalion was founded in 1910 and are a light infantry battalion. At first they were part of the militia and not a regular battalion. Their role is meant to be that of scouting and forming the screening forces in front of the main line infantry. The 'light' in the title refers to the speed of movement and that they carry light arms. In World War One such a distinction was not very clear. They arrived in France 1916 and were the only Canadian regiment to deploy with the same regimental and battalion number as the Canadian Expeditionary Force.

They are still part of the Canadian Army today.

Now for the first all arms badge for an army that was created *specifically* for action in World War One ONLY, and the badge is …

Canadian Expeditionary Force (CEF)

With the outbreak of the First World War the Canadian government formed the CEF to serve in this war. Ironically the Seaforth Highlanders battalion were initially refused permission to go to the conflict so many of the regiment volunteered for the CEF and left for Europe. Then the government relented and the Seaforth Highlanders were allowed to join the overseas forces. The CEF was composed of the full range of skills of a self-contained army. So this badge covers all aspects of what you would expect in an army. It was disbanded in 1919 when the war ended.

Kings Colonials New Zealand

Like the CEF, this force was created for the duration of the war only but this time it's a single regiment and our only yeomanry regiment. The yeomanry are part of Territorial Army and can be regarded as part-time cavalry.

This force was created in 1914 in London for New Zealand nationals living in Britain who wished to enlist with fellow New Zealanders. It was also referred to as the King Edwards Horse.

The regiment was dispersed when it was first sent to France with each squadron being attached to a different division before being re-united in June 1916.

There is a report that the last casualty was a private in C squadron. The regiment was disbanded in 1924.[1]

Australian Imperial Force

This badge is popularly referred to as the Rising Sun badge and was in use before World War One and has continued as the badge of the Australian Army. It has evolved over time and the one on the bedspread is the badge that was in use from 1904 until 1949.

As it is an army badge it is for all arms rather than a distinctive regiment or corps.

It was famously worn by the Australian and New Zealand Army Corps, the ANZACS, although the New Zealanders had their own, less well known badge. Yes, you go look them up. We've done a lot of the work already, haven't we?

And now the last badge.

South African Overseas Expeditionary Force (SAOEF)

Once again this is a hostilities only force.

It was General Jan Smuts who was the driving force behind the formation in 1915 of a South African expeditionary force to fight overseas as the internal Union Defence Force was restricted to home service only. These South Africans volunteers formed an infantry and artillery brigade but they never formed a contingent that was large enough to be an independent South African force. This way they were always part of a *British* Army division. And this was a fighting force for *white* South Africans only, all other races having to join the labour contingent and other non-combat units.

Like the other hostilities only forces we have mentioned, the SAOEF was gradually disbanded in 1919.

It might interest you to know that this badge also has another story. As you can see it is in Afrikaans and English and has the South African Springbok as its emblem. There is no reference to the British Empire on it at all – no coronets, crests or other clearly royal insignia. This was an attempt at the time to appease the bitterness of the Afrikaaners towards the British Empire following their treatment and defeat in the Boer Wars (1899-1902).[2]

Well that is the story behind the units that these badges represent but we still didn't know WHY it was made.

Chapter Three
We start our journey – in a lockdown?!

By now it was 2019 and we were pleased to hear of a great opportunity to try and find out more about it – the BBC 'Antiques Roadshow' was going to be filmed near us. We made arrangements so that we could go, hoping that we would be able to get some professional attention on it. BUT – it fell on the same day as our daughters School Leavers Assembly. THAT was far more important. We boxed the bedspread and placed it safely away. The mystery had to wait.

The bedspread was stored safely on top of our wardrobe in a purpose bought vintage wicker basket. We just never got round to looking any further into it as we are a fully functioning normal family who never seem to have enough hours in the day and are then too tired at night.

And then – 2020 and Covid-19 Lockdown hit the world.

I was furloughed and doing home schooling in the morning. Damian was able to keep working full time but from home. So, now we found we did have that elusive extra time in the day! This was our opportunity to research the bedspread as a family and give ourselves a morale boosting distraction.[3]

We now already knew who the regiments were. The next question we asked was:

WHY THESE TWELVE?

They are different countries, each had different expertise and each entered the war at different times.

We decided that the tank units badge would be a good starting place as they were deployed 'last' onto the battlefield in 1916. We did keep in mind that the bedspread may simply depict regiments involved in World War One. BUT that omitted many other British regiments and other nationalities such as the Indian, African and Scottish regiments.[4] So we looked up the Tank engagements from 1916 to then cross reference this list with the other 11 regiments actions and see if they were all active together somewhere.

One similarity did present itself – The Somme.

We are all familiar with the photographs and Pathe films of the Somme battle zone. The shells exploding and decimating the ground, the water and mud filled landscapes, the corpses littering the ground and the mixed living faces expressions captured by the camera.[5]

The Somme, or the Somme Offensive, is the bloodiest battle in warfare history. 1 July 1916 to 18 November 1916 was 140 days of ceaseless bombardment and carnage. It resulted in six miles of territory gain for the Allies and the loss of 20000 enlisted lives, the worst casualties occurring on the first day and the highest single day's loss for the Commonwealth forces.

Unfortunately, it was not a strong enough answer for the bedspread. Yes, these twelve all saw action at the Somme, but so did many other regiments and nationalities – Newfoundland, India, Bermuda, Rhodesia and France!

We were still stuck for an answer of why these twelve.

Chapter Four

Looking for one answer, we find another

Whilst looking for the answer in the previous chapter, we did find one definite piece of information – we could prove that the bedspread was made between September 1916 and April 1918.

The proof – the service records of the Tank Regiment and the Royal Flying Core. As mentioned previously, the Tank Regiment was first seen publicly in action in 1916. And the Royal Flying Core was renamed to today's Royal Air Force in 1918.

And it was definitely NOT made later than 1920.

The main reason we can be so confident of the 1920 date is because of the clue clearly visible on the Welsh badge. The word WELSH itself. At the Brecon based Royal Welsh Regimental Museum I was given the following information:

> *WelSh are the general term in use today. WelCh is the Old English version, the use of which declined from the mid-19th Century onwards.*
>
> *In 1831, an official document from the Adjutant General named the regiment as the Welsh Regiment of Infantry. The COPY of this letter, sent to the Officers of the Regiment, then serving in India, named them the WELCH Regiment of Infantry and they adopted this spelling. This resulted in a continued dispute until 1920. The War Office addressed them as the Welsh; the Regiment identified themselves as the Welch.*
>
> *Finally, Army Order No 56/1920 informed both the Royal Welch Fusiliers and The Welch Regiment that henceforth WelCh was to be used!*

So the fact that our bedspread has the S instead of the C helped to date it even more. Such a simple thing to establish and such an important fact in the development of the badges. Told you we didn't spell it wrong earlier.

However, we considered the possibility that it could have been made at a much later date as a World War One commemorative piece with the creators using the *historically correct* spelling and names of the regiments. One fact that makes this very unlikely though is the detail of the work and the time it would have taken to make it in the first place. Having done embroidery myself, I am very confident that this bedspread would have taken a *very* long time to execute, even if done full time and by a team of crafts people.

Chapter Five

A sign from above?

This dating of the bedspread was thrilling, and that it had survived so well and for so long in such a good condition. We took another good look at the bedspread itself. Was there any initial, name or something anywhere on it? It is white on white so it took some close scrutiny. Frustratingly, there was nothing. The only new clue it showed us was that the underside of the embroideries showed small signs of wear. The embroidered threads here were 'rubbed' and a little frayed so it had obviously been used for a time. BUT BY WHOM?! It made us frown by being such a conundrum.

Yet it also made us smile with enjoyment. Every time we looked at it we were amazed by the beautiful workmanship in it. This had been made by very attentive and skilled hands. We wouldn't describe it as a work of love but it certainly was made with immense dedication, care and time.

TIME TO DO IT – now there was a train of thought to consider; time, skill, materials, dedication, and *devotion* to task.

What about a religious order? Catholic Europe was not short of them. Ironically we had already come across a religious order whilst we were researching the badges of these WW1 regiments. The Royal Munster Fusiliers webpage recounts:

"In early December (1914) they (The Munsters) aided with the evacuation of the (Irish nuns) Ypres Benedictine Convent, whose occupants subsequently established Kylemore Abbey in Connemara, Ireland."

We thought this was a possible lead to explore. Fortunately this order did write a book about their forced flight from Ypres and this meeting is mentioned in the book.[6] The nuns recount how they met soldiers of the Munster Fusiliers returning from the battlefield whilst they were removing a cart load of possessions from their Abbey in Ypres to the La Sainte Union School in Poperinge. When the soldiers realized they were an Irish order, they proceeded to sing 'It's a long way to Tipperary' to them right there on the muddy road. The orchestrations of guns and explosions in the background must have been very odd! I also wondered if the nuns might have been bewildered at this serenade. Being a closed order, talking with men, let alone being SUNG TO by them, might have caused a few palpitations! They then gallantly 'escorted' the nuns to Poperinge.

An image of the rescue of the nuns from their bombed abbey by gallant Munster Fusilier soldiers appeared in the Dublin journal, the 'Weekly Freeman' on March 13, 1915. If you take both sides' accounts and the dates into consideration, it is a good example of how the press manipulated stories such as these to boost the morale back home.

But we digress –

Could this be a link to our bedspread? This closed community of Benedictine nuns and all these World War One regiments. The nuns would have seen the regiments in some capacity and they were known for their needlework. Their motto to this day is – "Work and Pray". The embroidery could be contemplative work; the linen is possibly Irish and the crochet lace border very ecclesiastical in our view.

We knew we had nothing to lose so we sent Kylemore Abbey an email. Lockdown meant we were probably in for a wait but the bedspread had already done so for 100 years, so what did another stint of time matter.

Chapter Six

Two steps forward and then one back

I have to confess that for a considerable time on this journey I had images of a Woman's Institute group making this coverlet. Maybe as a prize at a fundraiser during the war or as a commemorative piece after the war. Strains of 'Jerusalem' did fill my head at times. Similarly, the Ypres Nuns could have made it as one of the items sold at their Reparation Auction at the Goupil Gallery in 1922.

We seemed to have a lot of possibilities but no definite facts or information. Well, we did have one definite fact – the quality of the needlework. I was convinced that most of the work had been done by the same hand. I say most, not all, because in my opinion, one panel is 'flawed': the Australian Commonwealth Military Forces badge is not sewn straight or central on its panel. Was this needle worker less competent? Maybe a younger novice? A new group member? This was another fun detail the bedspread was silently throwing at us.

But one detail suddenly became very clear – Kylemore Abbey had **no connection** to it. Like the dates of their 'rescue' story in the press, another set of dates did not tally. The nuns were in England by late November, 1914, and the Tanks appeared on the battlefield in September 1916! The sisters would not have seen tanks in Ypres and so would have had no reason to embroider them. The nuns were out of the story. Typically this revelation came to us the same week Kylemore Abbey did get in touch with us. It was very disappointing for us to inform them that their information would no longer be necessary.[7]

Chapter Seven

We see a (very possible) light at the end of the tunnel

It was late evening and I was trying a few more search engines and put in "WW1 embroidery" and clicked on Images. 'Mystery surrounding Kiwi WW1 soldiers…'[8] caught my eye. I was tired but the clip was short so I pressed play.

Suddenly, I was not very tired anymore!

It was a report on the Altar Frontal Cloth of St Pauls Cathedral, London. It is beautifully embroidered by……. Wounded soldiers of WW1!

Our bedspread has

1) A military background

2) Made by needle workers with time

3) Made with dedication

4) The dates fit

5) THIS COULD EXPLAIN THE **DIFFERENT NATIONALITIES**

Chapter Eight
Shell Shock

In 1916 the British War Office noticed an increase in casualties of soldiers who had no physical injuries but whose characters were not coping with the battle being fought. It was diagnosed as caused by "a lack of moral fibre" and led to many sufferers being labelled as cowards. In 1915 the Lancet medical journal published an article by Charles Myers who emphasized the trauma the artillery shell explosions were causing to the human brain. Add to that the atrocities the person saw and the stress of the battlefield environment and it is clear the human brain could not cope. He highlighted the condition of 'Shell Shock', what we today know as PTSD.[9] Yet throughout the war the War Office actively discouraged, banned and censored any mention of it.

Myers advocated that the sufferers needed gentle coaxing back into society. He also recognised the need to *rehabilitate* those with life-changing injuries in the same way. If the disabled serviceman had a family but could not return to his pre-war occupation, the war disability pension came nowhere near to supporting them.[10]

Rehabilitation Therapy was founded, what we today also refer to as Occupational Therapy.

Many hospitals and convalescent homes took rehabilitation very seriously. Many devised workshops to retrain those whose injuries meant they could no longer do the work they had done before the war. 'Lap crafts' were devised to relieve boredom for those bedridden, or institutionalized, for long periods of time and other activities were to help with the exercising, and healing, of physical wounds. It also helped to make these men realize they still had a purpose in life, could contribute to society and earn a living when discharged. Some of these institutions included the Royal Brighton Amputee Hospital, Abram Peel Hospital, the Princess Louise Scottish Hospital for Limbless Sailors and Soldiers and St Dunstan's for Blinded Servicemen.

It was thanks to medical professionals such as Myers, Dr Arthur Hurst and Edgar Adrian[11] that it was eventually accepted by the military.[12]

Consequently, a lot of civilian Occupational Therapy initiatives came about too. These were clubs organised by the British Red Cross and professionals who volunteered their expertise to assist servicemen who had been discharged. It was a place for them to have a kindly ear, socialise and not feel judged ESPECIALLY if they had disfiguring injuries. They could also complete, or further, an education and learn new skills that could help them earn a living. But crucially, convince them they had a place in society.

Was our bedspread an Occupational Therapy item? This was going to be a new and interesting topic to explore.

Online searches helped us find the Lord Robert Workshop, the Disabled Soldiers Embroidery Industry (or Unit) and the Khaki Club.

The Lord Robert Workshop specialized in wood and metal working for toy manufacturing.

No link there then.

The Disabled Soldiers Embroidery Industry was created by Ernest Thesinger[13] who himself had served and was wounded in WW1. He took up sewing as a means of earning extra money whilst stationed in France. Post war he continued into embroidery and realized its merits to heal, improve moral and provide an income. This was a good possibility, not least because of the organisations title. They closed in 1955 but fortunately it had had a connection with an organisation still operating today and crucially had the DSEU archives: the Embroiderers Guild. We added them to our investigation list.

And then we looked into the Khaki Club. This particular one was established in 1918 in Bradford and interestingly was established *with* a hospital – the Abram Peel Hospital. This hospital specialized in neurology. Things were looking good. And its link with our search:

One of the rehabilitation classes offered was embroidery and it was taught by Louisa Pesel, only THE best embroiderer in the country at the time.[14] And again there fortunately is a present day link – the Embroiderers Guild.

It was formed in 1906 by graduates of the Royal School of Needlework. Both organisations were involved with Occupational Therapy courses in the First World War. And most importantly to us, both these organisations are still in operation today so might be able to give us some information.

Chapter Nine
Looking outside the main picture

Unfortunately we again have the issue about the different nationalities on the bedspread.

The twelve badges were all of different regiments and nationalities. NO World War One military hospitals or convalescent homes housed mixed regiments or nationalities! For example – South Africans were cared for in London, Indian regiments in Brighton, New Zealanders in Surrey and Essex and Irish ones back in Dublin.

This is the huge question we just cannot seem to answer!

So in the meantime, we tried a different tack. What about the lace border? There is 26 metres of it and frames the panels perfectly. It looks delicate but is remarkably strong. Did the pattern, hopefully, have a distinctive name or popularity? We contacted the Lace Guild to ask what kind of lace it was and if possibly this was a distinctive, maybe even a SPECIAL COMMISION, design? No such luck on the latter but they were able to tell us that it is called Filet Crochet, a mass produced lace made on a Barmen machine. Interestingly, the machine was developed in 1890 in the Prussian town of Barmen, now part of Wuppertal in North Germany but was in use in the UK in the 1920's and 30's. This information and the dates helped confirm the authentication of the bedspread which was a very helpful, and encouraging, result.

Chapter Ten

More answers please

By now we had decided to donate the bedspread once we were satisfied our research journey with it was finished. We don't have the right house for it and we have no 'connection' to it apart from some of the nationalities depicted. Also, neither of us had family that were active in any of the regiments depicted. We wanted to donate it to where it could be appreciated, and, hopefully, seen by the public. So our searches intensified knowing that if we couldn't prove its origin, we needed to collect as much factual and supporting information about it as possible. This would be crucial before museums or collections might consider accepting it.

If we could not donate it, as a TOTAL last resort, we would have put it in a specialist auction.

We decided to try and put articles in local papers and on social media to see if, ideally, the donor could be found or if anyone recognised it. We made it clear that we were not looking to return it but wanted any authentication and information. We also appealed to various national newspapers, online publications and television networks to run this story. It was picked up by our local Brecon and Radnor Express newspaper and the Brecon and Radnorshire Community Facebook also ran our appeal. We had no response of interest from the other platforms.[15] Although we received many comments of admiration about the bedspread, we didn't get the answer we really wanted – did anyone recognize it! It was disappointing BUT it also made us more determined to keep researching it.

Finally we contacted the Royal School of Needlework, The National Trust, The Embroiderers Guild, the Imperial War Museum and the Victoria and Albert Museum asking if they could give us any information and advice.

We knew that the lockdown did not guarantee any replies. All we could do was wait.

Chapter Eleven
We take a step back ourselves

In the meantime, we were having fun putting possible origin stories to it as information came to light and we found new lines of inquiry.

Here are a few we had so far:

- It had been made as a commemorative piece of a specific offense

- It was made to be a raffle prize at a war fundraising event

- It was made by a Woman's Institute group for someone

- It was made by nuns because of it being all white

- It was a product of an Occupational Therapy group and exhibited to raise funds

- It was meant for a grand house because of its size

- Because it is WHITE and double bed size, it was made as a wedding gift by a convalescing group for a special member of the medical personnel. The RAMC badge is top centre after all.

- It was made by soldiers convalescing at a requisitioned stately home as a 'thank you' for the home owners.

- It was made by an embroiderers group as a fundraiser prize

- It was made by embroidery colleges' students AFTER the war as an exhibition piece. During the war their time would only have been used making items for the war effort.

- It was made by a lady of a household whose family home had been requisitioned and this was her record of the regiments who had been treated. A sign of respect for them and a record of the family homes history.

- It came to the charity shop from a house clearance of someone with no family.

- If it WAS made by soldiers, we speculated that the Aussie/s who made the slightly crooked Commonwealth Badge got some playful ribbing – "Well, coming from down under, things must seem lopsided to you!"

We were getting a lot of pleasure from this very confounding, confusing, puzzling, international mystery. And interestingly it has never made us sad. We found that although we were confronted with horrible images and records on some parts of this journey, this bedspread is still a beautiful and calm item in our opinion.

I also realize that I have never mentioned its condition, apart from the slight signs of wear I mentioned earlier in the book. There is only ONE SMALL hole in the lace just to the right of the Canadian Expeditianry Force badge and only a few rust spots on the reverse of one panel. We suspect that it was used as intended on a bed and then put away, possibly when baby came along, and by sheer luck and good fortune it was put and 'forgotten' in a well-insulated loft, the back of an airing cupboard or the bottom of a lined linen coffer.

All these theories seemed VERY plausible.

Chapter Twelve

We are not alone

So we had gone ahead and contacted a few organisations to ask for help in our mystery bedspreads search. So far we had done most of the research ourselves thanks to the internet. With lockdown, communications were slow but……

Within 24 hours we were on first names with The Royal School of Needlework, the National Trust and the Embroiderers Guild.

Dr Susan Kay-Williams, Chief Executive at the Royal School of Needlework confirmed it WAS Whitework Embroidery. She also highlighted that this technique is only introduced to *advanced* second year students. So as we had already assumed, this was a very skilled and concentrated form of embroidery. She also confessed the bedspread confused her:

- there was so much of it, both in quality and detail

- the size of it of 180 cm by 230 cm. A double bed today is 135cm by 190cm

- that it was all white

In her opinion it was of the period 1916 to 1918 or shortly thereafter as she could not see why someone would do this much work in later years. Her confusion also lay in the lack of any names, dates or labels. Surely the maker/s would have wanted some form of signature on it. We shared her feelings and raised the BIG question – was it made by soldiers?

The Embroiderers Guild was also very helpful. Artistic Director Anthea Godfrey agreed the dates 1916 to 1920 made sense and that it possibly had links with a convalescent workshop and occupational therapy BUT also voiced the unusual feature that it was done in WHITE. Embroidering in colour would have been much more therapeutic! She suggested it may have a religious connection.

We were very pleased with their attention and information. It helped bring more insight into it and the hands that had made it. As we had no answers, we were happy to receive ANY kind of answer or research angle. As we listed in the previous chapter, a lot of avenues were open to us. One other exciting result was that both these organisations expressed an interest to accept it into their collections.

But we have to confess that at the time we had hoped the National Trust would give it a home. We had visions of it adorning a double bed or grand piano in one of their properties that had been requisitioned as a hospital or convalescent home in World War One or shortly thereafter. Unfortunately, Heather Caven, Head of Collections, was not able to consider it as a donation as it did NOT have a direct proven link to a property.[16]

And then the Imperial War Museum got in touch. Again, with no real provenance, they could not accept it into their collection but they kindly suggested two more organisations that could possibly help: The Museum of Military Medicine and the National Army Museum. We sent them the 'appeal mail' as we called it and again were ready to wait.

In the meantime we had had an automated reply from the V&A but none of the media outlets picked up our appeal. Never mind, we said. We still had something to get on with thanks to the information from the Royal School of Needlework, the Embroidery Guild and the Imperial War Museum.

Here I can also point out an incredibly telling fact: convalescing soldiers who were taught embroidery all had one thing in common – the first full piece of embroidery they were encouraged to make when they had been taught the basics was THEIR REGIMENTAL BADGE. After that, they were encouraged to do other patterns and pictures.

And then we got responses from the Museum of Military Medicine AND the National Army Museum. Both organisations were also as baffled as we were at its origin; reason for being made and by whom. Nevertheless both expressed an interest to take it into their collections regardless of this lack of answers. To say we were pleased was an understatement. We explained that we had had other offers too and would consider all of them when we were satisfied we had done all the research we could. All the organisations interested would then be informed so they would all know where they could access it.

Chapter Thirteen

A sobering possibility

Whilst we were digesting all the information we had so far on the embroidery, we realized it would be a good idea to look into the military hospitals that DID treat soldiers of different nationalities.

But first, we think it would be helpful to explain the process of evacuation of ANY casualty from the front:

A wounded soldier evacuated from the battlefield is taken to the RAP – Regimental Aid Post. Here he was treated to either be able to return to the fighting immediately or if he needed to be removed by a FA – Field Ambulance to the ADS – Advanced Dressing Station. If he was still too injured to be treated at the ADS, he was removed to the MDS – Main Dressing Station. The next stop was the CCS – Casualty Clearing Station. All along this chain he would be treated (such as bandages changed) and assessed at each 'Station'. If he needed to be moved along the line again, it was to a BH – Base Hospital. These were on the continent in places such as Dieppe, Le Havre and Le Mans, and as far away from the hostilities as possible so men could be treated to then return to active duty. If the casualty needed more, or longer, treatment, he was transported back to England. Here ALL CASUALTIES were first admitted to Receiving Hospitals, before finally to General and Auxiliary Hospitals suited to their needs and nationality.

Now back to our search –

We decided that our collection of nationalities could be mixed away from the battlefield in two places.

1) at a Base hospital BUT would they have been there long enough to finish it? We also had the image of a Head Matron disallowing the linen to be used as it would, quiet justifiably, have been necessary for bandages, dressings and bedding. Don't forget, base hospitals were on the continent, NOT in the UK.

2) a General or auxiliary Hospital that possibly also specialized in a specific PHYSICAL injury? Here nationality would not have had a part in the casualty's admission.

We decided to explore option two as it ticked the most of the 'yes' boxes to some of our questions.

So 'purpose built world war one hospitals for overseas wounded' was put into the search engine.

Netley Hospital, near Southampton, was the first hospital in England soldiers from the Western Front were evacuated to. Accounts tell how South Hampton harbour was black with the troop ships taking soldiers to the continent and bringing the wounded back. Three times a day the hospital ships would dock and a siren would sound at the hospital. All available staff would immediately organise themselves at the railway station to move the wounded, many still covered in the mud from the battlefield, to the receiving wards.

As this was a receiving hospital, the patients were relocated to other hospitals as soon as it was possible. BUT many did stay long term – and they were of all nationalities, even German prisons of war. AND occupational therapy embroidery was offered. An article headed 'Crippled Soldiers as Skilled Embroiderers' from the Daily Sketch dated November, 1916, shows Miss BH Shaw, Needlework Organiser, and Lady Emma Crichton, President of the Netley Handicraft Society, photographed at a needlework exhibition at Netley Hospital. The items were then going to Mrs Casalets home in London's' Grosvenor Square for exhibition and sale. Well, this was proof items like ours were made and got around the country.

Then we explored The Queen Hospital, Sidcup. Here soldiers from all the nationalities on our embroidery, as well as other nationalities, were treated for extensive and life changing facial injuries caused by the modern warfare German machine gun. This was a potential lead for two of our searches – mixed nationality AND a specific injury.

"The floodgates in my neck seemed to burst, and the blood poured out in torrents...
I could feel something lying loosely on my left cheek, as though I had a chicken bone
in my mouth. It was in reality half my jaw, which had been broken off, teeth and all,
and was floating about in my mouth."

John Glubb, hit by a shell fragment, 1917

Dr Harold Gillies, the man credited with being the 'Father of Reconstructive Surgery' was pioneering the medical procedures that were able to give thousands of men a chance at as near a normal life as possible. What is now often done as cosmetic improvement has its origins in the World War One hospitals where men had endured horrific injuries for the service of king and country. A sobering thought. Dr Bamji of the British Association of Plastic, Reconstructive and Aesthetic Surgeons, London (BAPRAS) and Gillies Archivist was also able to confirm that embroidery was an occupational therapy offered to the patients at Sidcup.[17] What a fantastic possibility for our bedspreads origin.

In Bath there was the War Hospital at Coombe Park that was SPECIFICALLY for overseas wounded servicemen. Volunteer Historian Alison Guerin at the Royal United Hospital, Bath, confirmed all our Nationalities were treated there, including American and Indian. And more importantly that occupational therapy embroidery courses were offered there. She also attached two newspaper articles of the period from the Bath Chronicle. The first, dated July 28, 1917, is a front page photograph under the headline 'Bath War Hospital Needleworkers' and shows a group of nursing staff and hospital patients, recognizable by their hospital suits, posing on a lawn holding panels of embroideries. UNDENIABLE PROOF! The second article, from Saturday, October 25, 1919, was even more exciting:

"Hanging at one end of the lecture room, where the exhibition is being held, is a
large bedspread, made by men in Wards 5 and 9 of Bath War Hospital for the
Premiers bed at 'Chequers', that beautiful residence which Lord Lee of Fareham
last year presented to the nation. It is a beautiful specimen of work. Another
quilt of similar order adorns an adjacent wall, but this is at present unfinished."

Alison Guerin was also able to show me a picture of a soldiers embroidery that is at Chequers today. That one has been classified as a wall hanging and shows twenty regimental badges done in their colours on a white background. It also has all the names of the needle workers and is emblazoned with the VERY useful information:

EMBROIDERED BY WOUNDED SOLDIERS REGIMENTAL BADGES OF OFFICERS IN HOSPITAL AT CHEQUERS DURING THE GREAT WAR 1914-1918

We were both delighted and jealous with this information.

Delighted because here was double proof that larger items like our bedspread were made. We are not forgetting the Altar frontal at St Pauls we discovered earlier but the majority of Soldiers Embroidery pieces are pillow covers, handkerchiefs, napkins, tray cloths and tea table cloths. Large items were very unusual as they took so long to make. Did their treatment time allow them to finish it?

Jealous because this one has all the facts and information.

BUT – as the Chequers one clearly states it was made there, could ours be one of the Bath ones! We are still in the game.

There are more hospitals we could mention but I hope you appreciate that we did as much research and explored as we could. Again, with no names or labels on our bedspread, we had no definite line of inquiry and were not going to get a conclusive answer but we were content to focus on possibilities.

Chapter Fourteen
Beneficiaries

During our search we came across interesting individuals who may have been the recipients of it. For example, in Nottingham, William Goodacre Player (of the Cigarette brand) donated generously to the Nottingham General Hospital.[18]

It could have been a gift for a member of a medical staff team such as Dr King Martyn. Along with Nurse Marjory Clark he is highly credited for his physiotherapy work at Bath War Hospital, also known as Coombe Park.

Again in Nottingham, the afore mentioned Sir Harold Gillies. From 1917 he operated on over 5000 facially injured soldiers. That is a lot of individuals who wanted to say 'Thank you'.

We just mentioned Lady Crichton and her Needlework Society and the society lady Mrs Casalet who offered her home in London to exhibit and sell embroideries to raise funds. (Did she buy one herself?)

Did skilled needle working French or Belgian refugees have a hand in making it? Maybe a group of such nationality nurses made it for a fundraiser or as a personal gift in their free moments to remember the soldiers they helped to nurse.[19]

Mayors, shop keepers, labourers, housewives, scouts, guides, vicars, professionals.......We could go on and on with all the individuals, from patriotic everyday people to people with influence and titles who contributed time and effort to fundraise for the war and support those affected in any way.

And we are not forgetting the millions around the world who gave their support to a conflict so far away.

Could our bedspread have been a gift for one such person or family?

Could it have been bought at a fundraiser sale or auction?

·Could it have been won in a fundraiser raffle?

Could it have travelled to a Colony and back?

We don't know but love imagining any one of these possibilities.

Chapter Fifteen

A secret is exposed

Earlier in the book, we hinted that there was a secret in the bedspread. Well, we are going to reveal it now!

In 1914 the Royal Naval Division was sent, on the orders of the First Lord of the Admiralty, (a certain maverick character called Winston Churchill – I wonder what happened to him) to try and relieve the siege of Antwerp. They deployed the armoured cars that were being developed, and although the action failed and Antwerp was captured by the Germans, it was seen that armoured vehicles could be vital as a war winning weapon. The British War Office continued to explore the use of armoured vehicles as a counter weapon to the German Machine gun. This work was initially carried out by the Royal Navy as they had the experience of armour and the use of turret mounted guns. The name given to the early trails was His Majesties Landships.

The British War Office was very keen to keep their development of these armoured vehicles a secret until they were ready for deployment. In the same vein, the early tank unit itself was also given a succession of cover names. These were:

In 1915 it was the Heavy Section Machine Gun Corpse. By August 1916 it was the Mechanical Warfare Supply Department and then the Heavy Branch Machine Gun Corp. This could have been a way of making it appear to the enemy that all these divisions were failing and being discontinued, making the British look incompetent, when in actual fact it was able to continue the development and training of these armoured cars.

To further keep the secrecy, the men being trained for the tanks kept the name of the regiments they were recruited from. These were the Motor Machine Gun Service and the Army Service Corps.

The Motor Machine Gun Service was a motorcycle and sidecar unit – one man drove the motorcycle and the sidecar passenger operated the machine gun. The Army Service Corps were responsible for transport, dispatch and administration logistics INCLUDING the supply of water, food and fuel.

The Mark 1 tank first appeared to the enemy on 15 September, 1916, at the Battle of Flers-Courcelette, as part of the Somme Offensive.

The British public back home saw the tank for the first time on November 23, 1916, when the Daily Sketch were permitted to publish images of it photographed on the battlefield.

BUT an *official* badge for the unit was NOT issued until July of 1917. AND THIS OFFICIAL BADGE IS **NOT** ON OUR BEDSPREAD!

OUR badge looks like the photograph that was printed in the newspapers in 1916! So it is highly likely the Tanks badge panel was started sometime between these two dates with the needle worker/s giving the unit its first official name among the forces – His Majesties Land

Ship Tank. When the official badge was issued, they decided to use the badge that had already been started – or maybe it had even already been completed!

Its impact on British morale was so enormous that it even inspired toys and ornaments, a handbag named 'The Tank' by Mark Cross and a song and dance called – what else – 'The Tanko'.

Chapter Sixteen
Was it them?

We decided to explore one more HUGE and very obvious feature – why was it all white!

I have already hinted that I found the lace border very ecclesiastical in look and after the advice from the Royal School of Needlework and the Embroidery Guild, we decided to see if there was a possibility it may have a Holy Order connection after all. We had already explored and (sadly) dismissed Kylemore Abbey so we turned our focus again on hospitals.

So we focused on hospitals, or at least medical stations, in religious establishments near the battlefield.

However – this is a complete non-starter.

It is VERY UNLIKELY our bedspread was made here during the conflict, these establishments being too busy with the fighting, nursing and war effort works. And the materials in our bedspread – the cotton and linen – would have been commandeered for use as bandages, wound dressings, clothing etc.

And if a religious institute made it AFTER the war, the needle workers would most likely have put in the official tank badge.

With no pun intended what so ever – the reason for its lack of colour was going to remain a blank canvas!

Chapter Seventeen
Over to you

In Chapter Eleven we listed our guesses about why it was made. We hope that by now we have convinced you that we really tried to find a definite story and that you are not disappointed that we cannot at the time of writing give a definite answer

We have now explored so much and hope that the journey will continue with you.

That I found this bedspread on the day after the 100th anniversary of the end of the First World War will always be significant to me. For Damian, that it was found when we were planning to entertain South Africans and Australians in Wales (and that he is Irish) and the bedspread represents these nationalities is an amusing serendipity.

Our journey with it will probably never end and we hope you will enjoy its possibly timeless mystery too. We have donated it to the National Army Museum in London and hope you will see it for yourselves and hopefully be as intrigued by its craftsmanship and mystery as we have.

Notes

(1) It was also a Masonic Lodge

(2) The Boer Wars were a series of conflicts between October 1899 to May 1902 between the British Empire and the white Afrikaaner farmers. They were predominantly of Dutch descent and 'Boer' is the Dutch word for farmer. This war ended with the conquest of the Transvaal and Orange Free State in 1902 and the violent suppression of the Boer Commandoes by the British. The fighting tactic of this war employed by the British was brutal but effective: they forcibly rounded up the Afrikaaner population and placed them in large camps where, due to mal-administration, many of the women and children died of starvation and disease. An incredibly harsh and inhuman British victory that to this day is still a very raw memory.

(3) This expression will become very significant

(4) An eyewitness in Belgium recalls her amazement when she saw the turbaned and bearded Indian regiment and then a kilted Scottish regiment being piper-led into her town. Think what these regiments must have thought of clogs and the flat landscape!

(5) A silent feature length film by Geoffry Malins and John McDowell was commissioned by the British War Office. The film mixed actual and staged scenes of the Somme battle and is today the most watched at the time and since film.

(6) 'The Irish Nuns at Ypres' DMC

(7) But we do now have a 'must visit' destination on our holiday list.

(8) Joy Reid report for NZTV, December 2018.

(9) Myers did not create the term 'Shell Shock'. His belief in the condition and his dedication to get it accepted by the War Office is a battle story itself.

(10) Other medical professionals believed in more forceful treatments and "knocking the sense back into them". Electric shock and ice bath therapies were promoted.

(11) Dr Arthur Hurst was a neurology expert. Edgar Adrian was a nerve specialist.

(12) Myers was so disgusted by his treatment by the War Office, he actively refused to co-operate in the Southborough Enquiry of 1922 into shell shock.

(13) Ernest Thesinger served in France. He was also an actor, appearing on stage and screen in England and America, most famously in "Bride of Frankenstein".

(14) Louisa Pesel was a celebrated embroiderer and textile designer. Commissions included written articles for the Victoria and Albert museum and embroidered items for royal households. She also became president of the Embroiderers Guild in 1920.

(15) In the following months, as we uncovered more facts we continued our proposals but it was not picked up. At least we can say we tried.

(16) We will still be renewing our annual membership though

(17) Gillies Archives

(18) His donation of £1250 in 1914 would be about £145184 in 2020.

(19) Over 200 000 Belgian, French and Russian refugees arrived in the UK from 1914 onwards. These were *able bodied people* who wanted to do their bit and despite the language barrier, took the jobs the fighting men had left. They also assisted in factories, some of them being ENTIRELY operated by them, and hospitals. When the war ended, the British Government offered them free passage back to Europe so as to make jobs available again for the returning men. Records show that by 1921, 90% of the refugees had done so.

ACKNOWLEDGEMENTS

Heather Caven, Head of Collections Management, National Trust

Alan Wakefield, Head of First World War and Early 20th Century Conflict,
Imperial War Museum

Teresa Pearce, Tirabad

David Singeison, Berkshire

Eve and Patrick Ward, Surrey

Sophie Ward, who originated the title of this book

Bath Records Office

The Alexander Turnbull Library and National Library of New Zealand

Sam Hall, Brecon and Radnor Express

Royal Welsh Regimental Museum, Brecon

Dr Susan Kay-Williams, Royal School of Needlework, Hampton Court

Anthea Godfrey, The Embroiderers Guild, Aylesbury

Jessica Ridge, Marketing and Communications, Kylemore Abbey

The Tank Museum, Bovington Camp

National Army Museum, London

St Pauls Catherdral, London

Museum of Military Medicine, Aldershot

Gwynedd Roberts, The Lace Guild, Stourbridge

Dr Andrew Bamji, British Association of Plastic,
Reconstructive and Aesthetic Surgeons, London

Alison Guerin and Hetty Dupays, Royal Union Hospital, Bath

Angela Conyers, Friends of Folkstone Museum

PHOTOGRAPHS

Battle of Courcellete
by Louis Weirter

Shannyn Johnson at the Canadian Army Museum, Ottowa

World War I returned servicemen embroidering, photographed by Leslie Hinge

Ref: PAColl-5932-27
Alexander Turnbull Library, Wellington, New Zealand

Altar frontal of St Paul's Cathedral, London, England

The Chapter of St Paul's Cathedral

Hollins Cushions

Dr Andrew Bamji – Gillies Archivist, British Association of Plastic,
Reconstructive and Aesthetic Surgeons, London, England

QUEEN MARY'S PURCHASES.
Articles made by soldiers at Queen's Hospital,
Frognal, purchased by the Queen and
Princess Mary at a sale at Chelsea House.

Dr Andrew Bamji – Gillies Archivist, British Association of Plastic,
Reconstructive and Aesthetic Surgeons, London, England

Territorials at Pozieres
by William Barns Wollen

National Army Museum, London

Tank lithograph
by Muirhead Bone

National Army Museum, London

RESCUE OF THE NUNS OF YPRES BY THE MUNSTER FUSILIERS, DECEMBER 1914.

Weekly Freemans, St Patricks Day, 1915

With thanks to The British Newspaper Archive. At time of press copyright holder unknown

Our son Joseph noticing the Welch badge matched the head of a two pence piece

Damian and Anne Ward